Animal Alphabet

Animal Alphabet

Richard Digance

with illustrations by Diana Gold

Michael Joseph . London

First published in Great Britain by Michael
Joseph Ltd
44 Bedford Square, London WC1
1980

ISBN 0 7181 1960 6

Filmset and printed in Great Britain by
BAS Printers Limited, Over Wallop,
Hampshire
and bound by Redwood Burn Ltd., Esher.

Contents

The Ants at the Olympics

At last year's Jungle Olympics,
the Ants were completely outclassed.
In fact, from an entry of sixty-two teams,
the Ants came their usual last.

They didn't win one single medal.
Not that that's a surprise.
The reason was not lack of trying,
but more their unfortunate size.

While the cheetahs won most of the sprinting
and the hippos won putting the shot,
the Ants tried sprinting but couldn't,
and tried to put but could not.

It was sad for the ants 'cause they're sloggers.
They turn out for every event.
With their shorts and their bright orange tee-shirts,
their athletes are proud they are sent.

They came last at the high jump and hurdles,
which they say they'd have won, but they fell.
They came last in the four hundred metres
and last in the swimming as well.

They came last in the long distance running,
though they say they might have come first.
And they might if the other sixty-one teams
hadn't put in a finishing burst.

But each year they turn up regardless.
They're popular in the parade.
The other teams whistle and cheer them,
aware of the journey they've made.

For the Jungle Olympics in August,
they have to set off New Year's Day.
They didn't arrive the year before last.
They set off but went the wrong way.

So long as they try there's a reason.
After all, it's only a sport.
They'll be back next year to bring up the rear,
and that's an encouraging thought.

Alan the Ape

Alan the Ape was dejected.
He was born without any knees.
He found it hard to ride horses
and harder still to climb trees.

He went to his mum and said, "Mummy,
it's embarrassing, help me out, please.
I can't jump, bend or do leapfrogs
with a stiff pair of legs such as these."

"Don't worry," said Mum, "it's your birthday soon",
and she patted her son on his head.
"We were going to buy you a tracksuit,
but we'll give you the money instead."

He went to the petshop and asked for new legs
and the shopkeeper said he had many,
so Alan took his coin and requested,
"Two Ape knees for a penny."

The Bear

When the Bear held a Fancy Dress Party,
just about everyone went.
Each animal went as another.
Well, at least that was the intent.

The Bat and Bull went as a Cricket
and the Bison went as a Bath.
The Viper sat on the Hyena's head
and they went as a laughing Giraffe.

The Eagle went as a Birdie
and the Birdie went as a Parr.
(A Parr is an under-aged Salmon,
in case you don't know what they are.)

The Panda turned up like a Penguin,
though he hadn't quite mastered the walk.
No one could tell the difference
when the Butterfly dressed like a Stork.

The Hedgehog turned up as a Buffalo
(Hedgehogs not being that bright),
but everyone said that he'd tried very hard
and he had an enjoyable night.

He almost came second for trying,
but it went to the Hippo instead.
He dressed up as a fairy-tale Unicorn,
with an ice-cream stuck on his head.

The Oyster, disguised as a jewellery box,
sang when his shell opened up.
A good try by Oyster but not good enough
to take home the Fancy Dress Cup.

The Skunk was most unconvincing,
sprinting in like a Gazelle.
It's hard for a Skunk to be anything else,
when they have that distinctive smell.

It was time to declare the Cup winner
and first place went to the Cat,
who covered his tail with red rubber
and hung from a tree like a bat.

Beaver the Believer

Beaver the Believer was swimming one day.
His family were talking but he'd nothing to say.
When, all of a sudden, he hit on a plan
and decided he'd build an incredible dam.

He had read in the Bible about a great flood,
so he gathered up branches, some twigs and some mud.
If it happened again, then he'd be prepared.
His wife, family and friends would be saved.

The other Beavers considered him mad.
His kids were embarrassed that he was their dad.
They said he should help them to work out their sums
and biting down trees wasn't good for his gums.

The Mayor of the River came down to inspect
this amazing construction so tall and erect.
The Mayor told Believer his building must cease,
for the Birds were complaining at the loss of their trees.

So thirty strong Beavers came down from the town
and together joined forces to pull the dam down.
Believer sat by the river and cried
and went to the sea where they say that he died.

Then down came the rains as never before,
the overcome Beavers were washed to the shore.
If only they'd never put Beaver's dam down,
his family and friends would still be swimming around.

So the Mayor told the King and the King told the land,
"Go out, you young Beavers, and each build a dam.
Build like Believer without a delay."
And that's what they're doing right up to this day.

The Bee

Bob Bee lived in a hive,
and in that hive Bob Bee would thrive.
He'd work all night and work all day,
but when weekends came he'd get away.
Oh, how he loved to be with flowers.
He'd sit and watch them dance for hours.
When night closed in he settled calm,
nestled in their pastel arms.
He met a golden daffodil,
her colour graced a forest hill.
She was taken from the forest
to be displayed by a city florist.
Her colours faded as she cried
but Bob Bee never left her side.
No one saw them through the glass
as they huddled in the florist's vase.
He never left, he never tried,
not until the day she died.
With city life she couldn't cope,
so she bowed her head and gave up hope.
Bob Bee is a lonely Bee.
Oh, such a lonely Bee is he.

The Bull and the Lamb

An overweight Bull strolled up to a Lamb
and said, "Please don't be afraid,
I know I'm big and I'm ugly,
but I can't help the way I was made.

"Allow me to introduce myself.
I'm a Bull and my name is Sidney.
Sooner or later I'll end up as steak
and it's possible you'll be a kidney.

"The way I see it, my dear little thing,
for us two there isn't a hope.
I will give you the ring from the end of my nose,
and to Gretna Green we'll elope."

Sidney is big with brown-coloured hair.
The Lamb is curly and thinner.
If they pass by, don't stop
them, don't try,
they're doing their best
to miss dinner.

The Cat

My Cat went to the pictures last night,
because he'd heard so much about "Jaws".
He thought he could make one more scary,
about a mouse-eating Cat known as "Paws".

A sort of a strong Tom and Jerry,
that's the general idea,
but in this one the cat is the winner
and the mice are just fur-balls of fear.

The producer just can't get the actors.
Mice are not that fond of pain.
As I heard one say as he walked off the set,
"I shan't fall into that trap again."

So if there are mice in your floorboards,
and it's highly likely there are,
tell them to nip up to Pinewood.
Tell them they could go far.

Cat and Mouse

The reason that we got a tabby, was to eat up the trespassing mice,
but Tabby's not keen on his duties, he says they don't taste very nice.
So they sit telling each other stories, and tell jokes about humans like me,
but I frightened Tabby this morning and I warned what the outcome would be.

I told him I'd get an alsatian and let it run free round the house,
unless he stopped thinking me stupid and severed his love for the mouse.
He said it was not in his nature, he hadn't the stomach to kill.
Besides, if he swallowed the head and legs, it would probably make him feel ill.

So I got the alsatian this morning. Tomorrow I'll teach it to beg.
At the moment it's completely unhousetrained and has just had a slice of my leg.
As for the cat and the trespassing mice, it was all sorted out fair and square,
the cat and the mice and alsatian, all sleep in my favourite chair.

It's cheese for the small ones, milk for the cat
and the big one is partial to steak,
and having never mastered the breaststroke,
I think I shall jump in a lake.

The Crab

A Crab gets fed up walking sideways.
It's got nothing to look forward to.
It keeps walking into coral and sponges
that its shell obstructs from its view.

A Lobster can see where it's going,
but always ends up in a pot.
So one of the queries of Nature,
is why a Crab looking sideways does not.

Needless to say, there's a reason,
they're not as dumb as you think.
They fit little mirrors on to their shells,
but it's hard buying mirrors in pink.

So they walk around looking like spaceships,
but it saves them a date with a cook,
and so long as they're free in the ocean,
they don't really care how they look.

The Crocodile

My little pet Crocodile is down in the dumps.
He's had a toothache for most of the week.
He's been brooding about with a sore, swollen snout,
and he's finding it painful to speak.

So I took him down to the dentist last night,
to see if he needed a filling.
The dentist proceeded to climb in his mouth
and in a minute or so he was drilling.

"Ouch," yelled Crocodile, "that really hurts,"
as the dentist drilled holes in his jaw.
He was half in his mouth and half hanging out,
so he went through his leg like a saw.

Crocodile told me he couldn't eat men.
I wish he had told me the truth.
The dentist, still drilling in Crocodile's head,
called out that he'd found the bad tooth.

"It's out," yelled the dentist with his very last words,
"No job is too big for me."
He then disappeared for the very last time
and the Crocodile finished his tea.

tooth specialist

Broken-Hearted Crocodile

Broken-Hearted Crocodile lived beside the River Nile.
The loneliest Crocodile throughout the land.
Little boys would laugh at him, never run away from him.
His tears turned to crystal as they fell upon the sand.
No one wanted Crocodile and so he left the River Nile,
headed for the open sea.
Every day he would swim and cry, wondering why he was
so shy and searching through his tears for company.

One morning, after years alone,
he met a friend who had left her home.
Together they would dance beneath the sea.
Two Crocodiles of high degree with mutual feeling lovingly
and seeing how happy life could be.
But broken-hearted Crocodile who lived beside the River Nile
was the largest living reptile ever seen.
He knew that it was not to be, so he left the open sea
until finally he came to Gretna Green.

People only laughed at him,
threw stones that barely broke his skin,
abusing him. He could not understand.
One morning as the sun caressed he gently slipped into
Loch Ness,
and with his broken heart he lived alone.
Some say he still lives in Loch Ness.
Some say he died of loneliness,
and others say he swam the open sea.
For broken-hearted Crocodile who lived beside the River Nile
just bowed his head and left most graciously.

So if you should see Crocodile, offer him a friendly smile
and tears will fall from saddened eyes once more.
Now not tears of loneliness but tears of long-lost happiness
and you shall be his friend for evermore.
Say, "It was so long ago, where have you been?
We've missed you so.
Why have you been travelling all alone?"
He'll smile and answer thankfully: "You never even laughed
at me."
With your loving reassurance he'll swim home.

The Dog and the Flea

Desmond Dog said to Fiona Flea,
"Don't keep moving, you're tickling me."
He scratched and he twitched,
he shivered and itched,
but love knows no boundary,
even for a Dog and a Flea.

Now Fiona had been with Desmond for years.
They met in one of the little pup's ears.
He scratched and he pulled.
She held on and called.
Nothing could separate
the love of the Dog for his mate.

When he rolled on the floor it hurt the Flea's head,
but she never complained, nothing was said.
He wagged and he shook,
but no need to look.
Fiona was still hanging on.
Their love was so binding and strong.

Then she left the Dog for a Hedgehog called Fred,
and Desmond gave his lost love up for dead.
Tail not a-wagging,
brown fur a-sagging,
Desmond wasted away,
never barking (he'd nothing to say).

One day as he strolled up the back garden path,
he met with the Hedgehog, knitting a scarf.
"Well I never, you're clever,
did you ever, nice weather."
They were talking in riddles and rhymes
when a Flea fell off one of his spines.

"Fiona," said Desmond, "Fiona, my dear,
I thought you were dead, but you're not, you're still here."
Crying and mumbling,
stalling and stumbling.
To be forever apart,
the Flea had broken his heart.

But the story's not over, for as Desmond fell,
he fell on her head, so she died as well.
The sky greyed, the sun stopped shining.
The Hedgehog sobbed (he must have been pining).
A love with no happy end,
was the Flea and her heart-broken friend.

The Dolphin

So near to understanding yet so far as oceans reach,
so trusting is the Dolphin . . . it remembers all we teach.
Just pray she doesn't understand our love is just pretend,
how we take away her freedom and still claim to be her friend.
Just like a ballerina, so graceful in the air,
if she really knew our reasons perhaps she wouldn't care.
But we can't fool her forever,
some day she will realise.
That's the day when the sea will belong to the fish
and the birds will rule the skies.

So lonely and so cold can be the distant sea,
but for miles she sails beside us, such loyal company.
So near to understanding as she smiles and disappears.
How I wish that I could tell her her friends will bring her tears.
Do you think we make her happy, performing like a clown,
travelling in a trailer and displayed in every town?
But we can't fool her forever,
some day she will realise.
That's the day when the sea will belong to the fish
and the birds will rule the skies.

The Duck

When you're a Duck like me it's impossible
to make friends with humans like you.
We're friendly and don't cause any trouble,
but you're not and you certainly do.

We swim round, me and the family,
while you throw us old lumps of bread.
Your dog starts to run with the crack of your gun
and one of us loses his head.

And if that's not enough, then you cook us
with our legs sticking up in the air.
Try putting yourself into our place.
I tell you, it just isn't fair.

The Egg

Eggy Egg longed for a leg
so on Saturdays he could play football.
He longed for arms to play tennis
and he wished that he was a foot tall.
But it's hard for an egg to be sporty.
They live within their shell.
They'd crack if they tried the high jump
and the hurdles are risky as well.
Eggy liked riding motor bikes,
but it's dangerous without any legs.
He tried it and started a fashion,
the first of the scrambling eggs.

The Flatfish

I wish I was a Catfish
and not a stupid Flatfish.
I wish that I could grow,
I'm tired of being low.

But on second thoughts,
not that fish.
I'd hate to be a Catfish.
A Flatfish to a Housefish.
Not a Catfish . . .
There's no Mousefish.

The Frog

In a brook that's quite near our house
lives a highly talented Frog.
He teaches tiny Tadpoles in their educational slog.
They stay all day until the sky turns grey,
and then they load their satchels and swim away.
It's the end of the day for the teaching Frog
so along the bank he jogs.

He's a teacher in the daytime
and he sings in pubs at night.
He dreams of being famous
and thinks one day he might.
He fills his lungs as he hums and strums,
while the Tadpoles sit and work out sums.
All except for Thomas Spawnleg,
who isn't incredibly bright.

At the local talent contest,
many thought Frog would win.
After all there aren't that many Frogs
that can play a guitar and sing.
He stood on stage, his guitar in tune,
and sang "By the Light of the Silvery Moon",
but as he reached the final verse
he regrettably broke a string.

How they laughed as his head fell slowly.
How they booed as he stamped in rage.
They yelled, "Crybaby Bullfrog",
as he stepped down from the stage.
All alone he took to the road
whilst on to the stage stepped a tiny Toad.
She played a piece by Mozart
which was very good for her age.

So Frog leapt homeward weeping
in the glow of the moonlit night.
He hopped upon his lily
and dreamt he'd won outright.
Second place, oh such a disgrace,
Frog could never show his face,
but he is practising for next year,
starting from tonight.

The Jungle Cup-Final

On Saturday, weather permitting, of course,
the Jungle Cup-Final takes place.
The Giraffes play Gorilla Athletic,
a rough crowd—a hard team to face.

The Gorillas know nothing of tactics or ploy,
they grab hold of the ball and they run.
They've played twenty-eight games since the monsoon last year
and so far they haven't lost one.

The Giraffes, on the other hand, count on their skills,
a sort of a long-necked Brazil.
They're sticking those necks out and saying they'll win,
but few think they actually will.

Their road to the final was merely a stroll,
in the first round they knocked out the Snails.
They had a second-round bye against Scorpion Town,
who kept bursting the ball with their tails.

In the third round they knocked out the Python eleven,
the Giraffes being fast and quite tall.
They played for an hour and ten minutes or more,
and only one Python headed the ball.

It was the high balls into the centre
the Pythons just could not match.
But hugging each other after the game
the Pythons broke two Giraffe's backs.

Athletic, too, had a far from hard run,
beating the Ants first of all.
It took ten million Ants to cover midfield
and a thousand to pick up the ball.

The second-round Lemming match, that was a farce.
Their goalkeeper climbed up the post,
then jumped off as soon as Gorillas attacked
and if he hadn't it could have been close.

So that's how they made the grand final today.
It's five minutes gone with no score.
A Gorilla's already been sent off for chewing
and by full time there could be some more.

Giraffes are attacking, it's two against two,
now Greg, their best player, is through.
Athletic close in and break all his legs
and the Gorillas sent off moves to two.

"Penalty," yells the capacity crowd
and Giraffes score a goal from the spot.
One more Gorilla goes off for dissent,
for he swore black and blue it was not.

Come half-time Gorillas are down to eight men
and not looking terribly pleased.
The Giraffes suck some lemons and sponge down their necks
while Athletic chew up a few trees.

The referee blows and the second half starts
and Giraffes get a goal from the start.
Two goals behind and three lads sent off,
the Gorillas begin to lose heart.

"Easy, easy," the spectators cry,
as Johnny Giraffe gets a goal.
A Gorilla disputes that Giraffes were offside
and swallows the referee whole.

The Elephant riot squad run on the pitch
to hold back the menacing crowd,
who were rather upset by Athletic's approach,
for eating the ref's not allowed.

The game was abandoned, Giraffes won the cup,
much to Athletic's dismay.
On the way home it was agreed that Giraffes
were the far better team on the day.

The Goldfish

Once I was a happy Goldfish,
swimming in the big blue sea,
until I was placed in a plastic bag
and a little boy won me.
He took me home to meet his mum,
who said with a caustic grin:
"Oh, look at him swim round and round
when I stick my finger in."

Every morning there's a big black cat
looking through the glass.
He licks his lips and then
he dips his paw in as I pass.
I think perhaps he likes me
and perhaps he's overfed,
and then I think perhaps
he isn't
and that soon I will be
dead.

A plastic diver came to see me
eighteen months ago.
He's supposed to be a real one
and they think that I don't know.
He landed upside down
and the paint's worn off his feet,
but he's better than the mermaid
they threw at me last week.

How I long to be in the ocean,
swimming in the mid-day tide,
with a lady Goldfish, fin in fin,
that I could make my bride.
A free-born fish I'll never be
until the day I die.
I'll just keep swimming round and round
and watch the world pass by.

The Greyhound

Mother Nature, I have a slight problem.
I think you have made a mistake.
It's sad because I know how hard you work
on the little creatures you make.
A Golden Retriever is Golden,
it's gold from its head to its tail.
The Red Setter is true to its title,
but here's where your categories fail.

Last night I discovered a Greyhound,
that was spotted and had a brown head.
So a spotted, brown head hound it should be.
But you called it a Greyhound instead.
To take it another step further,
the next Greyhound seemed to be white.
So the only feasible answer
is you named these creatures at night.

Mother Nature, you've made a slight problem
and you've certainly made a mistake.
If I was a black or brown Greyhound
I'd find it a bit hard to take.

The Halibut

Sally the Sole lived in the sea,
oh what a lonely Sole was she.
She loved a Halibut known as Hally,
but Hally wasn't pally with poor old Sally,
"I love you so," said Sally,
but Halibut wasn't impressed.
"You poor old Sole, what's wrong?" said the Whale.
So Sally the Sole confessed.

"I'm in love with Halibut, Hally doesn't love me,
I've tried and tried but his one reply is
'There's plenty more fish in the sea.'
I'd let him share my seaweed
and bring him worms for tea,
I'm in love with Halibut, Hally doesn't love me."

One day she met with a passing Cod,
who would best be described as an arrogant fish.
He said, "Come back to my weed and play."
Sally didn't dally, she said, "OK."
"Who needs Hally?" said Sally. "For as sure as a little crab nips,
I'd rather see him in a cat-food tin
or sitting on a plate with chips."

"I'm in love with Halibut, Hally doesn't love me,
I've tried and tried but his one reply is
'There's plenty more fish in the sea.'
I'd let him share my seaweed
and bring him worms for tea,
I'm in love with Halibut, Hally doesn't love me."

Sally thought Halibut wasn't aware,
and Hally pretended that he didn't care.
He gave a big fat worm to the sniggering Cod,
but the worm was on the end of a fisherman's rod.
Sally and Hally decided to marry
and things took a natural course.
As for the Cod he got sliced through the body
and sits in Parsley Sauce.

"I'm in love with Halibut, Hally doesn't love me,
I've tried and tried but his one reply is
'There's plenty more fish in the sea.'
I'd let him share my seaweed
and bring him worms for tea,
I'm in love with Halibut, Hally doesn't love me."

The True Story of the Hare and the Tortoise

Tortoise rose one morning from her sleep the previous night,
rubbed the sleep from out of her eyes and then switched on
 the light.
Bade the dawn good-morning, saw a letter by her bed
from the Hare across the way, which the Tortoise slowly read.
This is what the letter said . . .

Dear Tortoise,
 How are you today, isn't it a lovely day?
How are all your little friends that live across the way?
I'll make a challenge to you that I'll win fair and square,
A race of a mile, maybe two, round the meadow through the lair,
 Yours sincerely,
 Henry Hare.

Next morning as the sun rose they waited side by side.
Owl blinked and away ran Hare. Tortoise sadly sighed.
The race was on and Hare had gone, round Badger's field
 he came,
round the farmer's meadow, then round he came again
 (and again and again).
Then down came the evening rain.

So Hare made haste for shelter, into a burrow crept,
and as the hours slipped away Hare so gently slept.
But Tortoise kept on walking and with a finishing burst
crossed the line in record time officially placed first.
Hare awoke and how he cursed.

Tortoise won the trophy, which was placed beside her bed.
Hare lost face and favour and from the town he fled.
Every time you see Hare he's chasing here and there,
practising for next year's race that he'll win fair and square.
But Tortoise smiles and doesn't care.

The Huskies of Iceland

The ominous features of Iceland
are shrouded in luminous white.
The reason is to help out the huskies
that suffer from limited sight.
If the mountains were darker in colour
and not quite so blatantly bright,
the huskies would bang their cold noses
and stop making journeys at night.

The photograph below is of the ominous features of Iceland.

The Hyena

The happiest of the animal kingdom
are the Hyena and the Jackal.
The simplest joke or the strangest walk
will make these creatures cackle.
They're invited to all the animal parties
to get things moving along.
If the Hyena isn't laughing his head off,
there is something terribly wrong.

So how can you tell which one is laughing?
There's a simple answer, of course.
The Jackal tends to laugh in soprano,
whereas the Hyena's laugh is more hoarse.

The Jackal

Jackie was a Jackal who found it hard to cackle.
He couldn't even laugh when he looked at a Giraffe.
He found it sad to stare at a creature so high in the air.
Then one day out walking, he saw some hunters talking.
To hear such human madness ended Jackie's sadness.
As they sat together he heard them say how they were clever.
They said they were so hot, but clever they were not.
Upon looking Jack had never seen two so ill-equipped for weather.
When it rained they got so wet and in sunshine how they'd sweat,
and they toted loaded guns at helpless little ones.
Said Jack, "If they are clever, then I'm glad that I was never."
He watched them for a while, then went off with a smile.
The hunter and his chappie made Jackie very happy.
When he got back to the plain he started to explain
about the people he had seen at a place where he had been.
The Jackals squatted listening to Jack, his eyes a-glistening,
and soon they all were roaring at the two men out exploring.
Now Jack is a happy Jackal and he's often known to cackle.

Ken the Kangaroo

Ken Kangaroo came from Sydney,
and a champion jumper was he.
Young Joeys thought he was amazing,
saying that's who they'd grow up to be.

He could jump over trees and high fences
as if they didn't exist.
When they picked the Australian athletes
he was always top of the list.

One day he was reading the paper,
when a particular tale caught his eye.
Some horses were jumping at Aintree,
and he decided he'd give it a try.

He arrived where they hold the Grand National
and leisurely hopped round the course.
"Yes, I'll give it a go," said the Aussie.
A steward said, "What a strange horse."

The day of the race he was nervous
as he hopped his way round the parade.
He could see from the looks on their faces
that the horses were really afraid.

The crowd just couldn't believe it
as he made his way down to the start.
They wanted to laugh at young Kenneth,
but, frankly, they hadn't the heart.

The flag went down and they started
and the horses went down one by one.
A horse by his side smiled, and asked him his name.
"I'm Ken, and you?" "Oh, my name's Red Rum."

So Ken and Red went round together,
round Becher's and Valentine's Brook.
By the second time round Ken was tiring
and Red Rum was let off the hook.

Ken finally fell at Canal Turn
(in Australia they don't have canals).
If he hadn't he'd still be there jumping.
By now he'd be hopping round Wales.

A passing thought brought on by the total misunderstanding of the English language. It refers to the Kitten.

If a young Cat is called a Kitten,
then why isn't a young Bat called a Bitten?

The Koala Bear

The Koala Bear's reddish-brown
and he lives in trees, upside down.
The reason for the slight tinge of red
is the blood that's rushed to his head.

The Lemming

The life of a Lemming is one of no hope,
so as a Lemming please let me explain.
If, in reincarnation, I'm brought back to life,
I shan't be a Lemming again.

My wife, who has round about four kids a year,
has this year gone and had twenty.
We reached the point of starvation last night,
whereas this time last year we had plenty.

When such a happening happens we go
to help all our youngsters get by.
Don't think we go jumping off cliffs for a laugh.
If we didn't we'd starve, then we'd die.

So why do we have to go jumping off cliffs?
Why can't we climb down instead?
For those that survive swim into the tide,
but some don't because some land on their heads.

I'm a far better swimmer than some would believe.
I've a ribbon for swimming a length.
One hundred thousand left Finland last night,
and at the moment I'm round about tenth.

To be perfectly honest I don't want to go,
Scandinavia's been good to me.
I've led a good life and I have a good wife,
but now I must head for the sea.

Soon I shall die, for the ocean is wide
and that's what nature has planned.
Soon I shall join all my friends in the sky
and that's sad because I've just sighted land.

The Llama

The Llama's a jovial creature
that a book such as this has to feature.
It lives in the fields of Peru,
but these days there's only a few.

It can be compared to another,
because a Camel is a Llama's big brother.
A Camel's always complaining
about going somewhere where it's raining.

As for travelling for days without water,
the Camel don't think he oughta.
But a Llama just keeps a tight lip
and never lets naughty words slip.

So though they are similar in features,
they're completely two different creatures.
Although the Camel is down in the dumps,
a Llama never has humps.

The Moth

Geoff the Moth had a terrible cough,
so he headed south to shake it off.
But it's hard for a moth to survive,
living with an African tribe.

There's very few tribesmen wear clothing,
which meant little for Geoffrey to eat,
and he didn't finish the main course
(it was a man who had mud on his feet).

Next day he was out in the jungle,
writing postcards to Moths back at home,
when he came face to face with a Lion
who was biting the meat off a bone.

Geoff trembled so much he felt sea-sick,
seeing this ravenous beast.
"Don't be afraid," said the Lion.
"Come over and join in the feast."

"No thanks," said Geoff most politely,
"I'm afraid I only eat clothes."
"Well, is that a fact?" said the Lion.
"As it happens I've got some of those.

"This man was trying to shoot me,
so I patted him hard on the head.
I bent over to say I was sorry
and, lo and behold, he was dead.

"So feeling a little bit peckish,
I had a tug and a tear,
but I had to take off his trousers and coat
and I threw them somewhere over there."

"Oh yes," said Geoff, "I can see them,
and I rather fancy a snack."
So he chewed on the clothes for a minute or so
and then lay content on his back.

"Thank you so much, Mr Lion,
you've done me a really good turn."
"Don't mention it, Moth," said the Lion.
"To please is my only concern."

Then they became each other's best friend.
The Moth sat in Lion's left ear.
They set off in search of more clothing
and nobody's seen them all year.

A theory overlooked by Darwin in his Theory of Evolution, which if suggested could have changed the whole lifestyle of the mouse, causing major disruptions to the cheese industry and eventual starvation of the pussy-cat as we know it today.

If Fieldmice live in fields,
why don't Dormice live in doors?

The Nightingale

Nightingale, we must say goodbye.
I must turn as you take to the sky.
I know you have to go,
the cold winds came to tell you so.
But it seems so hard to me,
to accept what has to be.
I know the time has come
for you to follow the sun.
So take your place in the sky.
Goodbye, Nightingale, goodbye.

Nightingale, we must say goodbye.
We never spoke but we'd try.
You will be sky-bound in the hour,
where there's numbers there is power.
Join your feathered friends,
for every rainbow ends.
When the snow is falling
there will be no time for stalling.
You will never see me cry.
Goodbye, Nightingale, goodbye.

Some day when winter's passed
I shall hear your song at last.
Your friends will all be there,
the choir of Berkeley Square.
So as winter winds prevail
you must leave me, Nightingale.
As you cross the ocean
please don't think of my emotion.
I will see you by and by.
Goodbye, Nightingale, goodbye.

The Origins of Cricket

With regard to the origins of Cricket
there are many conflicting tales.
The sport begun as some back garden fun
when the Tortoises challenged the Snails.

An unlikely pair, you'd think to yourself
not being that fast or alert,
but cricket's not a very fast game
and neither side could get hurt.

The Captains tossed up, Tortoises lost,
Snails decided to bat,
it was hard to know which opening batsmen was which,
except one had a white floppy hat.

Neither side had a fast bowler,
so 'twas hard to know which team would win,
but Snails opened the score with a well-taken four . . .
. . . the wicket was not taking spin.

By lunch Snails had hit one hundred and ten
and both their openers had gone.
One was chewed by an Adder,
the other was caught at mid-on.

It's said in the sport that Tom Tortoise
is the best close fielder around.
He can run a yard in two hours
and his catching's remarkably sound.

So there he was up at the wicket,
Snails were on the attack.
Tom stopped a shot that was six all the way
and his shell got a very bad crack.

Due to Dandelions out on the boundary
the Tortoise field was quite deep.
Terry was bowling one ball ever hour,
so most had just dropped off to sleep.

It was soon quite apparent, despite their large size,
that the Tortoise attack was a failure.
Their biggest mistake was they hadn't used Jake,
a Tortoise of spin . . . from Australia.

So up he stepped with his definite style,
one claw each side of the ball.
It was met with a shot that had scored quite a lot
but this time scored nothing at all.

Snails were sure a single was on,
but after an hour hadn't crossed.
There seemed some sort of doubt . . . one was run out,
and another wicket was lost.

Sam Snail was in next and the field was perplexed:
He hadn't been bowled out for years.
But Tommy bowled short, Samuel was caught
and walked back to his team mates in tears.

Most of the batsmen were back in the grass,
it seemed like Tortoises' match.
Steve Snail had impressed with his vigour and zest
but was out to a very good catch.

By tea, Snails had scored two hundred and nine
and had one batsman left to go in.
An undersized Snail, called Freddy the Frail,
who looked most anaemic and thin.

Now Tortoises, thinking this could be it,
moved in to field close to the stumps,
but the ball left Fred's bat like a cannon
(the close fielders were covered in bumps).

For Fred, although looking quite skinny,
could bat like the devil possessed,
and what with banal Tortoise comments . . .
Quite frankly Fred wasn't impressed.

He hit fours, sixes and singles,
and was soon approaching his ton.
He played square to short extra-cover,
and his partnering Snail shouted, "Run."

Fred's running was certainly not his strong point,
his legs were as skinny as nails.
It just wasn't on, the run was too long,
and the Tortoises whipped off the bails.

"OWZAT!" yelled Tortoises, the umpire agreed,
and Freddie the Frail was run out.
He'd had a good bat and had it not been for that
he'd have made a hundred . . . no doubt!

So that was the end of the innings,
Snails got three hundred and one.
They started batting in August
and finished when Autumn had come.

So needing three hundred and two runs to win,
Tortoises started to bat.
First ball caught Tim Tortoise on the front of his claw
and the Snails as one yelled, "OWZAT!"

Now Sam Snail, who bowled from the Nursery end,
had many a pat on the shell,
but he wasn't content with one wicket first ball,
he wanted one on the next ball as well.

In came Terry, the Captain,
he was covered with scratches and scars.
As a man, I would guess, he would be a success
selling second-rate, second-hand cars.

Sam Snail ran and bowled to big Terry
and a Yorker caught Terry first ball.
"Not out," Terry said, and smacked Sam round the head
with his bat, which was terribly cruel.

How exciting, Sam on a hat-trick
and a very bad headache next day.
Two wickets had gone, Sam's bowling was strong,
and the third soon went the same way.

Three balls, three wickets, not one single run,
a really one-sided affair,
and the Tortoises feeling embarrassed,
put their heads in their shells in despair.

"Go for a draw, lads," yelled Terry,
to which the Snails replied, "What a cheek!
We batted all through the summer,
you'll be out by the end of the week."

And that's how the first Test Match ended,
the Snails made three hundred and one,
and Tortoises, most unexpectedly,
didn't get one single run.

Now as you know, Snails are not very big,
and too weak to go calling the score,
and they've got to live with the Tortoises,
so everyone called it a draw.

The Otter

It isn't surprising the Otter
thinks the Rat is a rotter.
People get them confused,
and that's when the Otter gets bruised.

They think they are one of the same,
and that leads to the Otter's great pain.
Although they swim with their nose,
only the Rat has got toes.

An Otter has got webbed feet
and his fur is spotless and neat.
The unsavoury sight of a Rat
makes you think it's been used for a mat.

No, it isn't surprising the Otter
thinks the Rat is a rotter.
People get them confused
and the Otter is not amused.

Who is the King of the Jungle? Some say the Tiger, some say the Lion. Some even say the Elephant. It's all opinion, but I know for certain who is King of the Forest.

Who is most feared in the Forest?
Who makes others scamper for home?
Some think it's the snake, but that's a mistake,
it's a wise old Owl called Capone.

The Penguin and the Puffin

The Puffin said to the Penguin,
"Why is it you can't fly?"
"I don't know," said the Penguin,
"I think I'll have a try."

He flapped and flapped and flapped again,
but still he couldn't rise.
"I wish I could," said Penguin.
"It must be lovely in the skies."

"It is, it is," said Puffin,
"you look down on lovely things.
It beats me why you can't fly too.
After all, you've got some wings."

"I know," replied the Penguin,
"but why I cannot say.
I wish someone would come along
and take the things away.

"I find it all embarrassing.
Like a fish that cannot swim.
If I found the chap that made me,
I think I'd murder him.

"On top of all that my feet stick out
and I find it a bit tricky to walk."
"So what are your good points?" said Puffin.
Said Penguin, "I can swim like a cork."

"I can't swim too good, Mr Penguin,
so you'll have to swim while I fly.
I'll keep up above you and look out for fish,
we'll be dining when evening is nigh."

So they searched for their dinner together,
the Penguin and his new friend.
They dined on a supper of Herring
and brought a nice day to an end.

So if you see Penguin out walking,
he's waiting for Puffin to call.
I know Penguin looks clumsy,
but he's basically having a ball.

Porky the Pig

Porky the Pig wasn't very big,
so he was not forsaken.
(He wasn't that much bacon.)

The Pike

In the rivers of England,
there are dozens of Pike.
They've all got long noses
and all look alike.
They all swim around in a big-headed way
and eat all the small fish
that get in their way.
They're just like the prefects
that went to my school.
No time for the first stream at all.

They're the biggest of all
the freshwater fish,
and the scarcest too
is many's the wish.
They never tell jokes
or have a good laugh.
They only smile when they bite fish in half.
No wonder they're hated
from river to stream
by the Roach, the Rudd and the Bream.

If they're caught by an angler,
the other fish clap.
They yell, "God bless that man,
what a wonderful chap."
The rod stops bending,
the line runs slack.
They've spoken too soon.
The beast has come back.
"Three cheers for the Pike,"
and they all clap once more.
They're frightened just like before.

The Queen Bee

She sat on her throne made of honey,
doing nothing but counting her money,
she dreamed of flying the Atlantic
or doing something romantic.

Her workers drew her a map
and she sat with the map on her lap.
She gave her crown to a reliable fellow
and dusted her gown of black and yellow.

She took to the sky alone
with not so much as a drone.
As she wiggled her wings,
she looked down on beautiful things.

"It's nice," she said to herself,
"and it's very good for my health."
But no sooner had she spoke
than she was covered in London smoke.

She coughed and lost her direction
and soon she caught an infection.
Somewhere over Wapping
her wings were close to stopping.

Oh, how she longed to be home,
humming content on her throne.
Her Kingdom was miles away,
so Queen Bee called it a day.

A Sparrow approached the Queen
and said, "Your Majesty, where have you been?
Your subjects are concerned
and their worrying seems confirmed."

He placed the Queen on his back
and passed over chimney and stack.
The Queen could hardly speak,
being so tired and weak.

As he passed, the other birds said,
"Watch out, there's a bee on your head."
But the Sparrow stuck to his task,
and returned their Queen, just as they'd asked.

It must have been a quarter to five
when they arrived back at the Hive.
The Bees whistled and cheered
(the news not as bad as they'd feared).

The Sparrow was given tea
before he went home to his tree.
It's nice to tell stories like these,
the tale of the Birds and Bees.

The Quetzal

It's sad the Quetzal's not famous,
because it's a beautiful bird,
but it comes from the Aztec regions
(from where very little is heard).

Now if the Quetzal had come from Watford,
a Trogon from Hertfordshire,
we would all know what it looked like,
but as it happens we've got no idea.

It's a bird with a beautiful plumage
and it's colours are vivid and strong.
To me it sounds like a Parrot,
and we've got them where I come from.

It's sad the Quetzal's not famous,
because it's a beautiful bird.
And should you like winning at Scrabble,
then Quetzal's a beautiful word.

Q
P
CAT
SHOT
UP
UETZAL

The Rabbit

Rabbit said to kind-hearted Whale,
"Will you find me if someday I'm lost in a gale?"
After he'd nodded, the good Whale replied,
"If I'm chased by a fox, will you help me to hide?"

The Racoon

Once there lived a Racoon
who was rather good at pontoon.
He was the richest Racoon around.
Some say he'd won over a pound.

One day a Toad known as Croaker,
offered to play him at poker.
Some animals travelled yards
to see such a contest of cards.

The Racoon almost resigned
when Toad opened with three of a kind.
It was exactly what Croaker had planned,
to open with a very strong hand.

Racoon was as quiet as a Mouse
as Croaker put down a full house.
He was just about to back out
when Giraffe gave a disgruntled shout.

"Because I've got a long neck,
I can see Toad is stacking the deck."
Toad said that it just wasn't true
and that the cards which he used were brand new.

The animals threw peanuts and booed.
They thought Croaker's tactics were crude.
Cheating each other was wrong,
so they told Toad it just wasn't on.

They sent him off to the pond,
or the swamp or where he belonged.
He tried to argue instead,
so a Hippo sat on his head.

Needless to say, for Toad,
that was the end of the road.
When Hippo got up off the floor,
Toad's head was incredibly sore.

So he limped off back to the swamp
(which you'd think would rhyme with damp).
But it doesn't, so now, my friend,
this poem has reached its end.

The Rhino

It's said that the home of a Rhino
is covered with layers of lino.
That's because his manners are poor,
and he drops his food on the floor.

Charlie the Salmon

Charlie was a Salmon from Scotland,
he could leap over fifteen-foot walls.
I'd like to explain how he came to his end
attempting Niagara Falls.

He met with some fish on migration,
some huge North American Trout.
They'd come for some quaint English jumping,
but hadn't seen that much about.

"Not much about?" said our Charlie.
"You shoal of ungrateful things.
I could show you some rocks up in Scotland,
to get over you'd need pairs of wings."

They just laughed and patted his head with their fins,
which made Charlie Salmon turn red.
They said that the best place for Salmon like him
was between two slices of bread.

That hurt Charlie Salmon so he boldly replied,
"I'll outjump you all . . . name the rock."
They yelled back, "Niagara . . . and you can go first."
Then muttered, "You big-headed Jock."

So later that month they were gathered.
The home team wore maple-leaf red,
and Charlie the flag of St Andrew,
with a crash helmet strapped to his head.

Charlie looked up at Niagara
and nervously cried, "Where's the top?"
The crowd replied, "Just keep on flapping,
if you don't it's an almighty drop."

So he disappeared into the torrent
with his crash helmet, goggles and map.
And the last words spoken by Charlie
were, "Somebody turn off the tap."

The One-Eyed Snail

There was a children's bookshop at the corner of the town.
No one ever went there, for they thought it had closed down.
There, an old librarian, bespectacled and all,
dusted down the antique shelves of stories yet untold.

There was an ageing volume with its cover worn and frail,
within its pages untold tales of Sam the One-Eyed Snail.
By night he slept beneath a tree beside a river dam,
by day he wandered through the woods and in the river swam.

Autumn came and brought the rain, leaves began to fall,
and from his tree, Sam could see beyond the dam so tall.
The water rose above his toes and Sam began to think:
There's a hole somewhere I must repair, for if I don't, I'll sink.

So Sam he swam along the dam until he found the leak,
and seeing that it was his size and that the dam was weak,
his bravery surpassed his strength and he squeezed himself inside,
and in that hole, so damp and cold, our Sam the brave Snail died.

No one knew Sam had gone from the town beside the brook.
No one ever passed the dam and no one read the book.
But when the shop is painted and those dusty books are sold,
everyone will read of Sam that One-Eyed Snail so bold.

The Stickleback

Here's the story of a Stickleback, known as very little Jack,
who lived in a municipal park.
His body was so little and his bones were rather brittle
and he dreamed of growing up to be a Shark.
But he knew it was impossible when others who were horrible said,
"Little Jack, you haven't got a chance."
And Jack's greatest wish of all, to meet a fish so beautiful at the
Municipal Park Pond Dance.
But nobody danced with Stickleback,
everyone he asked said no.
Nobody danced with Stickleback
at the Municipal Pond Disco.

So little Jack the Stickleback, under rather rude attack
from all the other fishes at the do,
swam around on his own, oh so dejected and alone,
knowing he'd never meet another 'til he grew.
The months they came and past and Jack grew up at last,
and soon got all the whistles and the glances.
It was plain to be seen Jack was really Jacqueline
and the nicest little mover at the dances.
But nobody danced with Stickleback,
everyone he asked said no.
Nobody danced with Stickleback
at the Municipal Pond Disco.

Now to dance with Jacqueline was every fishes' dream
and they clamoured for the glamorous sight.
But she only had an eye for the Sticklebacks and fry,
much to their surprise and their delight.
She told them all the truth of her disappointing youth
and how her size had caused such trials and tribulations.

"Now everybody queues, at a dance I pick and choose,"
and the Sticklebacks all yelled, "Congratulations."
But nobody danced with Stickleback,
everybody he asked said no, no, no.
Nobody danced with Stickleback
at the Municipal Pond Disco.

Yes, there once was a Stickleback, known as very little Jack,
who lived in a municipal park.
He was so afraid of Pike and Water Rats alike,
he only did his swimming after dark.
He knew little fish like him, although underweight and thin,
were tasty as an early morning snack,
and he knew at a dance he had very little chance,
so he minded his own business at the back.
But nobody danced with Stickleback,
everyone he asked said no.
Nobody danced with Stickleback
at the Municipal Pond Disco.

The Turkey

Turkeys don't like Christmas,
which may come as no surprise.
They say why don't human beings
pick on people their own size.
To sit beside potatoes
in an oven can't be fun,
so a Turkey is quite justified
to feel he's being done.

Supreme Turtle

A Turtle is a middle-class Tortoise.
The Tortoise should be equal, it thinks.
For whilst the Turtle goes swimming,
poor Tortoise tries hard, but he sinks.

You never find Tortoise in restaurants.
Eggs and soup show Turtle's class.
Middle-class big knobs eat Turtles
but Tortoises only eat grass.

To the Turtle's desirable mansion
the tenement Tortoise looks pale,
but the Tortoise can find consolation
in the shabby abode of a Snail.

Snail rents a bedsit, a Slug is the same,
while a Hedgehog's cottage is thatched.
Tortoise would only have cause to complain
if it found its house, one day, detached.

The Weasel

By its speed you would think that the Weasel
was running on petrol or diesel.
I'd like to confirm that it's not.
Four legs is all that it's got.

Its closest relation's the Stoat.
It has a summer or warm winter coat.
And if snow should be in sight,
it has a waistcoat of white.

The origin of Weasel's not clear
but I think I have an idea.
From all that continuous running,
the Weasel feels wheezy and done in.

The one thing left to confirm
is the story, as children, we learn.
It runs but forgets how to stop,
and that's when the Weasel goes pop.

William Davidson Whale

William Davidson Whale lived at the bottom of the sea.
No one sent him birthday cards
or dropped by to offer him tea.
He had no close-to-heart friends,
he lay alone in his bed.
As the evening hours passed by,
the tears rose out the top of his head.
Poor William Davidson Whale.

How embarrassed he felt
when the little fish called him names.
They jumped on his back and made wisecracks
and never let him join in their games.
He sighed, "Oh deary, deary me, I'm the clown of the big blue sea.
I've got no room in this world anymore,
there isn't any home for me."
Poor William Davidson Whale.

So it came to pass that all the world was at war.
A submarine hit William's head
and Willie wasn't certain what for.
A torpedo tickled his tail,
making William a most disturbed Whale.
He began to cry, "I don't want to die,"
when suddenly there blew a strong gale.
Sad William Davidson Whale.

A British ship nearby appeared to be in distress.
He scratched his head and then he said,
"This is my chance to impress."
Chancing the raging seas, and holding some plastic trees,
the sailors thinking he was land
climbed on, then fell to their knees.
Good old William Whale.

When all had climbed on board,
he yelled, "Full steam ahead. Three cheers for Winston Churchill,"
then for England William sped.
The sailors, feeling dazed,
were most understandably amazed,
and for bravery on the big blue sea,
William Whale was praised.
Good old William Whale.

Now no one laughs at him, the fish no longer dance.
It's said that William does no harm
but no one seems to give him the chance.
The fish don't call him names, he has medals pinned to his tail
and as he swims they clap their fins for William Davidson Whale.

The Woodworm

Robert was a matchstick
with a little dark brown head
that he would dip in water
before he went to bed.

Robert loved a Woodworm.
They seemed a perfect match.
But when kissing, Worm got splinters
and hugging made him scratch.

Never play with matchsticks.
Be wise, you little Worms.
The moral of this story is:
Remember Robert Burns.

Worm and Worm Limited

Two Worms were sat on the pavement one day,
when one said to the other, "We must get away.
Let's walk a few miles, get a London address.
We'll go into business and be a success."

The Worm that had listened was quite unimpressed,
thinking the other had spoken in jest.
"What chance do we have? We will never be great,
we'll just sit here till someone collects us for bait."

"Wrong," cried the first Worm and tried to explain.
"We shall make the little Worm mighty again.
I'll be a Bookworm and you be a Glow
and we'll hire ourselves out at a fiver a go.

"For all the people that read books at night,
I'll keep their places and you give them light."
Worm and Worm Limited that day was formed
and the smallest company ever was born.

The Yak

Kay was a Yak that was backward,
that's why she was called Kay.
She lived in Tibet (in the mountains),
till her employment caused her to stray.

Now, Yak are like Oxen with long hair
and not seen too much in the wild.
So the slow ones get caught by safaris
and Kay did when she was a child.

She was spending some time watching climbers
climbing up well-trodden rocks,
when, before she could say "Mount Everest",
she was caught and slung in a box.

The lid came off in London
and she found herself in the Zoo.
The Jackals couldn't stop laughing
and the Elephant said, "What are you?"

"I'm a Yak," replied Kay, quite disgruntled.
"Anyway, you're one to talk.
What are you doing with that leg on your nose?
You must find it tricky to walk."

"It isn't a leg," said the Elephant,
"it's a trunk for eating my food,
you scruffy excuse for an animal."
Kay replied, "Don't be so rude."

So Kay went to see the Zoo barber
and now she looks just like an Ox.
The people stopped stopping and gaping,
so they packed Kay back into the box.

Now she's back at her home in the mountains,
and when the other Yak pass by they laugh.
For their hair measures twenty-four inches,
but Kay's is an inch and a half.

ZOO
REJECTED

Debra the Zebra

Debra the Zebra went out for a walk,
to show off her colourful dress.
She strutted around like a film star,
but nobody seemed that impressed.

"I'm not impressed," said the Hippo.
"I'm not impressed," said the Snail.
"I'm not impressed," growled the Tiger.
"Nor me," blubbered the Whale.

She was heckled and jeered by female Giraffes
and scorned by sections of Llamas.
They said she looked like a Donkey
in tasteless, dazzling pyjamas.

Debra the Zebra thought for a while
and said, "Yes, that's certainly true."
Then she turned to the giggling Llamas,
saying, "That's strange coming from you."

"A Llama is short of spectacular.
In fact, you're a horrible sight.
I don't care what I look like," said Zebra.
"At least I can keep warm at night."

The Zoo

If you don't believe these stories are true,
why not go on a trip to the Zoo?
Mention this book and you'll be classed as a friend.
Give them my love. This is the end.